W9-CDX-425
3 1242 00225 2584

m 196 (8/14) ②

Community

The Grocery Store

by Heather Adamson

amicus
readers

1

Amicus Readers are published by Amicus
P.O. Box 1329, Mankato, Minnesota 56002

Printed in the United States of America at Corporate
Graphics, North Mankato, Minnesota.

Library of Congress Cataloging-in-Publication Data
Adamson, Heather, 1974-
  The grocery store / by Heather Adamson.
    p. cm. -- (Amicus readers, My community)
  Includes index.
  Summary: "Describes a shopping trip to the grocery store,
including various departments such as the bakery and deli.
Includes visual literacy activity"--Provided by publisher.
  ISBN 978-1-60753-027-5 (library binding)
1. Grocery trade--Juvenile literature. 2. Food industry and
trade--Juvenile literature. I. Title.
  HD9320.5.A33 2011
  381'.456413--dc22

                                        2010011110

Series Editor   Rebecca Glaser
Series Designer   Mary Herrmann
Book Designer   Bobbi Wyss
Photo Researcher   Heather Dreisbach

Photo Credits
Andersen Ross/Getty Images, cover, 19, 21 (t); Cathy
Yeulet/123rf, 13, 20 (t); Chuck Savage/CORBIS, 11, 21 (m);
Corbis/Tranz, 17, 21 (b); Janine Lamontagne/iStockphoto,
1; Jupiterimages/Getty Images, 5; Nicole Ward, 7, 9, 20
(m, b), Slobodan Djajic/Shutterstock, multiple pages
(watermark); Steve Skjold/Alamy, 15

1223
42010

10 9 8 7 6 5 4 3 2 1

Contents

Let's go to the grocery store. With help from the workers, we can find groceries for our picnic.

In the bakery, Dan the baker makes fresh bread in big ovens. We can get some bread for sandwiches.

bakery

7

Lynn the butcher wraps up chicken for us. We will cook the meat on the grill.

butcher

We need deli meat for sandwiches. In the deli, Ben weighs ham for us and puts it in a sack.

Grocery stores have rows of food shelves called aisles. We will find crackers there.

aisle

13

The dairy section has milk, cheese, and yogurt. We buy some cheese for our sandwiches.

Last, we stop at the produce section. Li brings us some apples fresh from the orchard.

produce

Time to check out.
The cashier scans
the prices. We pay.
Now we're ready for
our picnic.

cashier

Picture Glossary

aisle—a walking space between rows of shelves

bakery—a shop or part of a store that sells baked goods like bread

butcher—a person who prepares and sells raw meat

cashier—a person who scans the prices for items and collects the money

deli—part of a grocery store that sells ready-to-eat meat, cheese, salads, and sandwiches

produce—things that are grown and harvested such as apples and carrots

The Grocery Store: A Second Look

Take a second look in the book at the photos to answer these questions.

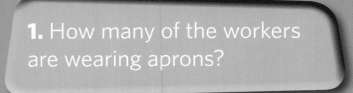

1. How many of the workers are wearing aprons?

2. What shapes does cheese come in?

3. What is the blackboard special at the meat counter?

Check your answers on page 24.

Ideas for Parents and Teachers

My Community, an Amicus Readers Level 1 series, provides essential support for new readers while exploring children's first frame of reference, the community. Photo labels and a picture glossary help readers connect words and images. The activity page teaches visual literacy and critical thinking skills. Use the following strategies to engage your children or students.

Before Reading
- Ask the children where they get their food.
- Have children tell some of things they see at the grocery store.
- Look at the picture glossary words. Tell children to watch for them as they read the book.

While Reading
- "Walk" through the book and look at the photos. Ask the children to guess what they think they think is happening on that page.
- Read the book to the children or have them read independently.
- Show children how to use the features of the book, such as the photo labels and picture glossary.

After Reading
- Ask the children about the last time they went to the grocery store. Did they visit all the places in the book? What in the book was the same as and what was different from their grocery store?
- Talk about ways to get food other than from the grocery store, such as growing your own food in a garden or going to a restaurant.

INDEX

WEB SITES

Kids Clubhouse—Healthy Minutes: Supermarket Safari
http://www.iptv.org/kids/healthyminutes/SupermarketSafari.cfm

MyPyramid.gov USDA For Kids
http://www.mypyramid.gov/kids/index.html

Supermarket Adventure: PBS Kids
http://pbskids.org/arthur/games/supermarket/supermarket.html

ANSWERS FROM PAGE 22

1. three
2. rectangle, square, circle, and half circle
3. lamb chops